Laced In Love

Jesselyne Abel

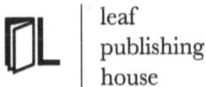
leaf publishing house

ACKNOWLEDGEMENTS

I'd like to thank you all. Special thanks to my parents, my brother, and Atiba Nurse for constantly supporting, motivating, and being my blackboard for ideas. Thank you to my friends and poetry family with all the kind words, support and advice. Thanks to Adil Dad and Leaf Publishing House who spotted me on Instagram and provided me with this opportunity.

Thank you all, for seeing and igniting the spark in me when at times I didn't see it in myself.

Love is the addiction
That binds us together
That keeps us alive
And yet we are always searching for it

Table of Contents

Love of Self *7-28*

Love of a Partner *29-72*

Love of Life *73-104*

Love of the Spirit *105-124*

Love of Self

I'M WORTH MY CROWN

Gone are the days
Where my head's not raised
And wonder fogs up my brain.

Now are the times
Where the sun rays shine
Where my smile is bright
And my crown is finally placed.

SUNKISSED FREEDOM

At this moment
As the sun beams down my face,

Making my enriched melanin
Gleam like one of God's wonders,

I am free.

SHINE THROUGH EMPTY

For years he filled my empty
And I his,

Two separate entities on a journey
Found love under sheets
Where their copper tones
Glistened like Earth gems
And hearts no longer broken

But right now
Though my heart's repaired
Traces of empty reopen
So small my face doesn't show it
And now I embark on a journey
Trying to shine in the midst of it.

BLOSSOM

And as the flowers bloomed
Her fog lifted
And she began to live.

SERENE

Enclosed by the misty blue
I am serene,

One who is with self.
One who is free.

Exposing the lens
Of my true identity.

With curls wild and free
Embracing my Venus,
Releasing my royalty.

REVIVE MY GROWTH

I was a bag
Of mixed emotions
Disguised as smiles and laughter
That suppressed my inner demons
Whose hyena like voice chuckled
At my misery.

A bag of mixed emotions
That was shown through my timidity
While silent tears hit the floor
Cleaning my soul
Washing away the pain
Reviving my growth.

TANGLED THREAD

I ripped the tangled thread
That's holding these broken pieces
That's holding in the pain
That's preventing me to heal
That's preventing me to live
That's preventing me to be me

LOVE YOUR INNER CHILD

It's ok

To love your inner child
To take yourself on play dates
To hide under pillow forts
To be in a box and imagine
To draw outside the lines
To scream and cry in pillows
To run across fields
To scrape every part of you
To take a nap
To have an open mind
To be blunt
To observe and wonder

It's ok
To love
And to love you.

ONE'S STARE

I have a love
Or lack thereof
Of the person before me.

I stare at my coffee colored eyes,
An entrance to all emotions and my soul.

I stare at my full lips,
A pathway for words to be music to one's ear.

I stare at my deep copper tone skin,
A beauty so bright it's imitated by others.

I have a love
Or lack thereof
Of the person before me.

I stare at my scars
Healed wounds that are simply reminders of my failures
Stare at my mistakes, shortcomings, empty promises.

I stare,
Even though mama says not to
I stare.

I stare,
In love with the person before me.
With everything she lacks
With everything she has
For she is beauty in the eyes of her Maker.

VOICE OF SILENCE

There's a calmness
As she stands
Overlooking the valleys below

Each mounted
By Lego brick houses
Filled with the silence
Of people talking – but not listening.

Inhale…
Exhale…

Closing her eyes
She begins to see

To taste,
To hear,
To smell,
To feel,

To Be.

MELANIN

They say
Beauty is in the eye of the beholder.

But why is it
That one class that one beholds
Was the definition of beauty.

I didn't realize
Didn't want that side to socialize
You had to hide
You had to blend.

Your beautiful pigment of skin
OUR largest organ
Yet mine viewed as dirty.

But I've come to realize
It's no longer the magic trick
Meant to disappear!

So shine!
As I wear you with pride
I wear you with delight
I wear you because you are me

The past
The present
And the future to be.

BLINDING BEAUTY

Stop and stare at a mirror.
Stop and stare at a mirror.
Stop and stare at a mirror.
And still can't see my beauty.

FREE PUPPET

Crafted by a puppeteer
I listened in my inner ear
To voices that society knows,
And I go. And I go.

But soon
My nuts and bolts,
Begin to rust
And the strings that held me
Turned to dust

And those voices,
I no longer trust.

Now I run like Forest
Finally Free...

To explore me.

LET IT RAIN

It's the rain
That grows
The seed inside of me.

The seed that lights me
The seed that guides me.

And my feet
Rooted on solid ground
Igniting my crown
Releasing my beauty
That's been found.

BEING

Be in love
With being still
With being one
With being whole
With being

ACCEPT WHAT'S WITHIN

Did you change?
Or did you just become who you truly are?

BORN OUT OF WATER

She was born
Out of a colorless, transparent life
With moonlight illuminating
Her skin.

And as the moon
She waxes and wanes
Sometimes full, other times empty.

Though her feet remained planted
On the cocoa soil
Enriching her with nutrients
Of what it takes to be

Woman.

TRAPPED IN FANTASY

Gently you had me drifting
On a plane of subtleness
Towing the line between
Reality and Delusion.

You had me so far gone
I thought words and actions were synonyms
And every whisper serenaded
Lulled me to false security
Pillow talks morphed
Fantasy and reality.

Slowly walking me into darkness
Trapped in the sunken place
Until I awakened
My inner voice
And found the key
To be free.

FINE ART

Your presence
Is fine art.

Your entrance
Heard without an utter of words.

Your spirit
Shines through darkened souls.

Your aura
So bright, you cease to be human.

You are a masterpiece.

Love of a Partner

FIRE SPARKS

Fire sparks
Decorate the night
With sweet gusts of warmth

Lined with pearls of hope
And you the center piece,

Staring up at me
For the long-awaited kiss.

TRAVEL THROUGH ME

With closed eyes
And an open heart
Drifting off in memories
Till our horizons meet
Into a harmonic sunset
Captivating our souls
Into surrender.

VINYL

You had a vinyl soul
A never-ending record
Of smooth jazz melodies
Mixed of needle pierced scratches
That mimicked the harmonies in mine
And from it our story was composed
Into song.

PLAY YOUR SONG FOR ME

As I lay my head upon your chest
I listen to your unreleased song
Protected by the cage of time.

Playing the song of your people.
Playing the song of your sorrow.
Playing the song of your highs.
Playing the song of your tomorrow.

As I lay my head upon your chest
And listen to your song
I hope you edit me into your lyrics
Because you are where I belong.

QUICKSAND

Your
Kiss is
Soft, velvet quicksand
Sinking me into your
Fire

LET NIGHT FALL

Let the lights go low
And fall with me,
Dwell with me,
In oblivion.

BLESSED KISS

They say when your heart stops
You are officially dead –

No longer in the physical
Transcending to the spiritual

So know when we kiss
And you feel my heart skip a beat

Know every time,
For each moment
You transcend me
Out of this world
And into the heavenly realm
Until another kiss
Brings me back to reality.

AS WE KNOW IT

A reflection,
Showed blurred pixels of herself.

With each one drifting into the
Expanding, electric, eccentric universe.

Knocking on the doors of
Not so familiar souls,
Obsessively hoping one will
Welcome a piece of her in.

Intuitively attaching herself,
To the one, who sees her full reflection.

LOVELY BEGINNINGS

Besides
Every love that is
Gained,
Is a
Never-ending soul connection.

SHE RESTED.

When heaven opened,
　　Her soul lifted.

LOVER'S RELEASE

Drench your inner thoughts
Into my being
While I take your pain away.

UNKNOWN LOVE

Thank you
For teaching me
How not to love.

NAKED LOVE

Love me when I'm vulnerable
So you learn to love me naked.

LUST

She jumped into passion
And drowned in despair.

YOUR MY EROS

I look at
Those brown eyes
And soft smile.

You staring down at me,
The sun rays gaze your cheek.
I can lay here for a while
Your arms holding me close
Feeling your breath on me
Got me hypnotized, child.

And your whispers got me melting now
I lay here as if I'm on white clouds
With blood racing, my heart's going wild.
Electricity, in me flowing
And our memories, they are rollin'
Of the times, you and I, all compiled.
Oh man, I love your tender kisses
For you are my Eros, I am Venus
My love for you will never be mild.

MOON RIVER

Sometimes
When my thoughts are a little spacey
And I stand at the mouth of the Moon River
And walk alongside,
I make sure after all these years
Our stars are still connected.

PERSONAL POTION

Your lips are the medication
Your touch the vibration
Electrical impulses spreading.

I linger for more
Heart-thrilling,
Mind-racing,
Episodes of day to day living
In your arms.

ONE

Just like clouds come with the sun
And stars with the moon
You and I are one
A bond that can never be undone.

HIS LOVE

And he comes with a presence
That tickles my skin
That makes me smile
That fills me up
That makes me whole
That is by my side
That let's me know I'm not alone.

LOVER'S RIB

Different day
Different time
You and I created separately

On the same timeline, he knew
You and I would meet eventually.

Didn't rush
Didn't push
Just knew what was expected

Others maybe jealous
Yes, I found a love where I am cherished.

One thing that I know for sure
Is the truth of Genesis 2:22-24
That out of your rib God created me
Two jagged puzzle pieces, fitting perfectly.

LOVE FIGURE

The shape of her silhouette
Against the sun beam glass
Is engraved in my memory
A love I once had.

YOU

You are not just a person
But a home I'd like to make
A world, I'd like to explore.

STORYBOOK

Lay me down
Like a story book
And read my body
As an autobiography
Told only to you.

Memorize my lines
Caress my curves
Gaze into my eyes
And travel to a whole new world.

REDAMANCY

With brown colored eyes, he stares at me
A beauty so pure, it hypnotizes me
A kiss on lips so sweet,
Dwell in redamancy.

RESTORE
Restore: to bring back to existence

Be mindful
For you did not restore me.
For I was already pre-designed on the Earth.

Creating a light in me that blinds
your dimmed mind.

So you use a diamond sharp tongue
To try to cut then repair me.

Be mindful
For you did not take my existence .

I exist.

Until my heart beats its last love
Until my last word shines from above.
And you don't have a hold on me.

For you did not take my existence
For you did not take my
For you did not take

For you did not take – me.

MELT ME

Melt my insides
Melt my mind.

Melt my heart
It's divine.

Melt with whispers
Melt with words

Melt my being
It's all yours.

HIS VOICE

From his voice
She knew,
She was loved.

PILLOW TALK

Meet me
Where the sun meets the sky
Where the moon meets the stars-

And gaze into the horizon
And lay on pillow clouds
And think of all the possibilities

Of us.

KISS ME LIKE THIS

Find someone whose kisses:

Calms the mind
Tickles the spine
Melts the soul
Makes you feel whole.

COOL PALM AND TICKLING KISS

I stood in front of you
With cool palms
And a mind full of wonder
A tender smile
With tickling lips
Ready for a kiss
And then I wake
From this fading dream.

UNSPOKEN HEALING

He speaks the words
She longed to hear.

She heals the pain
He's held for years.

LOCKED WORDS

My words, are the language
Of unsaid feelings
That takes the shape of daydreams
Morphed into the unfelt and unseen
Buried deep in the pits of my soul
Kept with a lock and key
Searching for my locksmith
To understand and unlock me.

BETWEEN CROSSHAIRS

Meet me at the spot
Between now and the end
And let's stay there forever
Trapped in the crosshairs
Of love and time.

10-106 (SECURE)

Your love
Is like a bullet lodged
In me -

Too delicate, too risky to remove
So you stay in me
Become a part of me
A physical memory yet,

I learn to live my life without you.

GARDEN OF EDEN

Come
With me
In my garden
Of Eden- learn to

Live

TELL ME MORE

Kiss me in the dark
Sublime concoction of love
Oh those summer nights

GEM

Know that my body
Is the vessel of my soul
A raw, uncut gem

SOULFUL AROMA

Somewhere we will meet
Where the aroma of our souls
Takes me on a hidden trail to you.

LOVE LIKE THE MOON

Love stamped on the heart
Moon stamped on the daybreak sky
Permanent shadow

RAW

Stare past my outer
Past my baggage
Past the heavy loads of anxiety
Past the whisper of my insecurities

Stare at my raw
Raw power
Raw confidence
Raw emotions I will no longer shield
Raw love
Raw beauty.

Stare at me.

RECIPE OF AMOUR

It's that stare
You give me
In dimmed light,

That has:

1. ½ cup of fears and worries
2. 4 tablespoons of shades of black
3. ½ cup of dreams and hope
4. 1 cup of awe and delight
5. A pinch of sugar and spice

Baked in my soul
Drizzled in our journey
Garnished in our future tomorrows

This is the recipe of Amour.

FOREVERMORE

I want to know
That you just don't
Love my body -

But that you love
My soul.

For it's my soul
That lives forever.

Love of Life

FOGGED REALITY

We feel as if we are just passing through
Going through the motions
Searching for a new
Underneath the mystique
Of reality.

UNTOUCHABLE FEELINGS

Ever think about how
It's the words that we whisper
It's the beat of the music
It's the soul in the song
It's the touch of the wind
It's the warmth of the sun
It's the hurt in the tears
It's the crease in our faces-

It's the untouchables,
That brings out memories
That makes us anew
That binds us together

And that is when
We truly feel.

GRAND LOST SOULS

We are always in constant motion
Even when we try to be still
Our mind is racing
Moving faster than the hardware we stare at
Hardware we created and wear on our sleeves
Showing the world our true love
Is ourselves…

And we continue to move
Trying to find a home for our lost souls
Never thinking a home is already found
We just have to stop moving
And stare at the grandness
Of our world.

BLUE STREAM

It's the night
That captivates us.

The midnight blue
Streamline our thoughts
With crystalized wonder
Strung along the sky
Interlaced with glistening hope
Of our tomorrow.

MOTHERLY

Out of her breasts
Pours the sweet nectar
Milk and honey.

And we drink her:

Promises

Strengths

Powers

Burdens

Sacrifices

Pain

Tears

Love

HOMEBOUND

Small reflected glass
Paint the night sky.

Each given a name,
That matches our soul.

Guiding us on our path
Back home.

LET'S MAKE A PICTURE

I am a dot.
Connected –
With other dots
Trying to make a picture out of life.

NOT SORRY

If sorries
Were currency
Then many payments
Will be fraudulent
For we lack the heart
We are given.

BIRTHED

She birthed humanity
Surrounded,
By her love colored essence.

Lined,
With gold and silver ancestral markings.

Providing,
The power that's within her.

Exalting,
The ones who pushed before.

Strengthening,
The one that is within her.

Until it's time
To be born.

LIVED BEAUTY

Staring at a looking glass
His mind begins to see
Painted figures on his face
Telling life freely.

Every worry, every smile
Edged in wrinkles of time
Every memory, every mole
Captured the secrets
Of his soul.

Staring at the looking glass
The man begins to see
That his long-lived face
Is quite a beauty indeed.

XENO
Xeno: the smallest measurable unit of human connection typically exchanged between passing strangers.

Walking along the highline under the sky
Passing by, exchanging smiles in our eyes
Connecting on the soul plane,

Until gravity brings us down
And the heartbeat of xeno dissipates.

SECOND

It's quick
A flash before our eyes.

We take advantage
Of every minute it builds.

Schedule a time slot
Hour by hour
Wishing we had more in a day.

Yet to our dismay.

Distractions
Are
Yielding
Spineless moments.

Compounding
Into 365
Where more and more mesh
Into slabs of a year.

And all we take for granted
And all we seem to only remember,

One Moment. One Flash.

RAINBOW SPECTRUM

Between our natural
Lens
Incapable of viewing
Nothing but shades of grey
Dimmed to our
Eyes of
Darkness

Colorblind man sees
All the rainbow spectrum
Splattered on bodies – sharp neon colors
Matching our soul.

LIT

Walking down the street lit sidewalks
I awake and see

        Life expands

        Inserts my soul into its milky swirl

        Tosses me into the horizon.

DROP OF MEMORIES

Gaze outside
And watch the rain drops race,
Down the window pane.

Think of all your memories
And all the ones there are to gain.

POWER OF THE TONGUE

We are the authors of our stories
Every chapter, every memory
Every word on the page are words we utter
To our friends, to our enemies.
So let's watch how we speak
For some words we cannot untweet.

CPR

Constantly cruising
Constantly pacing
Constantly racing.
Never ceasing
To enjoy the moments
Between the tick and tock
Until we need to breathe.

SINGING DAISIES

White daisies poke through
Rough, dry cement.
Singing-

One more chance to rise
Once more chance to be
One more chance to smile,
Since darkness only lasts a little while.

SUNSET DROWNING

Deep in the depths of my emotion
Sinking further and further down
Pulled into the world of

Past.
Present.
Future.

Grasping at the glistening crimson rays
Being shown the truth

Of loving,
Of living,
Of being.

HUM

Nature's vibration
Echoes in our soul
Mesmerizing song.

WOMB OF CREATION

Life starts in the room of creation
Rests on our glass marbled Earth,
Yet we think we rule every nation
Until one day, we will get what we deserve.

MINI MILKY SWIRLS

Surrounded by milky swirls
Sparkling beams of light explode
Into depths of undiscovered, unknown, unseen
To our naked eye and mind.

Yet we fear and not believe
We are held in hands of the creator
And only revolve,
Around our own mini swirls.

SHINE UP ABOVE

And when you go
Please make your way
Among the stars
I stare at up above
So I know your always there
Shining and guiding me.

ASYMMETRY

We were made asymmetric
In order for us to see duality
Of ourselves and surroundings:

- An in sync, complex unity

EMPTY CANVAS

From birth
We are nothing but empty canvases
Waiting for life
To paint our picture.

REOCCURING BEGINNING

As the night falls
One chapter comes to a close.

And when the stars appear
One chapter starts to be told.

REMEMBER LIGHT

Even in the darkest depths of the ocean
There is life…

So remember, even in your darkest moments
There is light.

DROPLETS

Let each syllable be droplets
And have my words rain
On you like springtime,

Filling your atmosphere
Of mist and freshly cut grass
Taking you back to innocence

Drenching your heart to emote
What you've kept hidden
What has you shaken
Has your mind tracing each droplet
On it's windowpane -

And now you see life.

AN ARRAY

Its with a calm mind
Life expands and shows itself
An array of colors

MY STORY

I try to write my story
Without words but with:

Capitalizing the rays of sunlight
Spacing out moments for reflection
Fight the fear of the unknown
Yet enjoy the sound of being still,
All while smiling through the track of my tears
Telling my story as one long run on sentence until …

The end.

Love of The Spirit

TAKE ME WITH YOU

She asked: What do you see in my eyes?
He said: Your journey

SUNDAY'S PERSPECTIVE

I bring life and light
To a world whose aura
Is filled with shades of grey.

If only you knew
How my light bends
For you to see
How my deeper color reflects
And learn from a different perspective.

SILENT PRAYER

Even though her prayer
Was filled with inaudible emotions,
He heard every cry.

FAITH

*Faith
Is believing
In the unseen
Yet feeling what is real*

FORGIVENESS

Forgiveness
Is the silent weapon
that KILLS them but,

HEALS you.

GENESIS

Darkness falls
Thoughts echo and swirl around
While his voice remains still
And whispers …

It's a new beginning.

SANITY

Here lies :

Scintillating
Soul

Searching and

Never-ending
Midnight thoughts

Of hope.

SILENCE SPEAKS

Sometimes what needs to be said
Is nothing at all.

BEYOND

Off into the distance
Beyond the borders
Of our mind.

I see into the future
Beyond our current time.

I say this to my sisters

> Chin up
> Fix your crown
> Shine from within.

I say this to my brothers

> Chin up
> Fix your crown
> Be the leader that's within

Off into the distance
Beyond the borders of our mind.

I see that everything the light touches
Can be mine.

ANCESTRAL WOMAN

Eyes closed
Strength drawn from within
As her ancestors hymns
Travel through her veins
Filling her afro textured crown
With knowledge that is embedded
In her spirit-

Passing wisdom
From generation to generation.

LOVE ENTERS

There's a moment in time
When hands touch slightly
Then interlace like spider webs

When hearts race
Then melt like ice cream

When eyes look into each other
Then shine bright like the hottest star

When the mind is on
Awakens the soul
And love enters.

INSPIRE

Ignite a
Never ending
Soul Snatching
Purposeful
Idea and
Resurrect
Everyone.

SOULFUL PLANE

Love
Is when
Two eyes meet
On the soulful plane
Connecting

NOT IN THIS WORLD

I stare blankly
Off into the distance
Escaping the physical
Entering the ancestral land
Energizing my spirit
Trusting intuition
And in a snap released.

ARISE THE FORGOTTEN

In gray ambience
Ground your roots, one with your soul
Lift the forgotten

ILLUMINATE

Sometimes
I stay outside at night
For it's then, I hear your voice
And your soul illuminating
The moonlight

TEARS SPEAK

The words that I speak
Mimic the sound of my tears
Echoing my soul.

LOVE CONNECTION

It's installed in us
Downloaded from a forgotten time
Traveling silently
Searching for it's partner

But you see it in the eyes
You hear it in the words
You feel it in the touch
You smell it in the air

And you just know.

I hope you have made this journey through love.
And its many forms.
I hope you have found love.
I hope in some way my words mended a broken piece
And you felt my love for you.

And with this tale at its end,
I have the two most important words for you

Thank You

ABOUT THE AUTHOR

Jesselyne Abel received her degree in biology and works in the healthcare field, but has been writing poetry since she was seven years old. At first it was her break from structured writings like essays, then it became a hobby and an outlet. Now, it is a way to share her message in the hope of making an impact on others. Some of her work can be found in "And We All Breathe The Same Air" a poetry anthology. To contact her and view more of her work, she can be found on Instagram *@ink.jess.*

Laced In Love
First Edition
Copyright © Jesselyne Abel 2020

All Rights Reserved
No part of this publication may be reproduced
without written permission from the author.

ISBN: 978-1-8380331-3-2

www.ingramcontent.com/pod-product-compliance
Lightning Source LLC
Chambersburg PA
CBHW021441080526
44588CB00009B/639